Contents

Buccaneers and corsairs were other names for pirates

Buccaneers were pirates from the Caribbean Sea. Their name comes from the word 'buccan', a wooden frame they used to smoke fish and meat on the island of Hispaniola.

Corsairs, like the Barbary corsairs from North Africa, raided ships and ports in the Mediterranean Sea and North Atlantic Ocean. They had fast galley ships that used oars as well as sails.

Lots of things
you want to know about
PIRATES
...and some
you don't!

Written and illustrated
by David West

W
FRANKLIN WATTS
LONDON•SYDNEY

First published in the UK in 2014 by Franklin Watts

Franklin Watts
338 Euston Road
London NW1 3BH

Franklin Watts
Level 17/207 Kent Street
Sydney, NSW 2000

Dewey classification: 910.4'5

A CIP catalogue record for this book is available from the British Library.

ISBN: 978 1 4451 2716 3

Franklin Watts is a division of Hachette Children's Books, an Hachette UK company.
www.hachette.co.uk

LOTS OF THINGS YOU WANT TO KNOW ABOUT PIRATES ...AND SOME YOU DON'T!
David West Children's Books, 6 Princeton Court, 55 Felsham Road, London SW15 1AZ

Copyright © 2014 David West Children's Books

Designed and illustrated by David West

Printed in China

The pirates' flag was called the Jolly Roger

Most Jolly Roger flags had a skull and crossbones on a black background. They were flown to frighten other ships into giving up without a fight.

Many pirates designed their own Jolly Roger. Calico Jack Rackham had crossed swords instead of bones. Blackbeard flew the devil spearing a red heart.

Pirates' ships were small and fast

Pirates used small ships called sloops and caravels. They were fast and agile. This meant they could catch the slower trading ships, filled with treasures.

The pirates' small ships had a shallower **draught**, so they could dart up shallow rivers and **creeks** to escape the large, navy warships that were sent to catch them.

Some pirate victims were forced to walk the plank

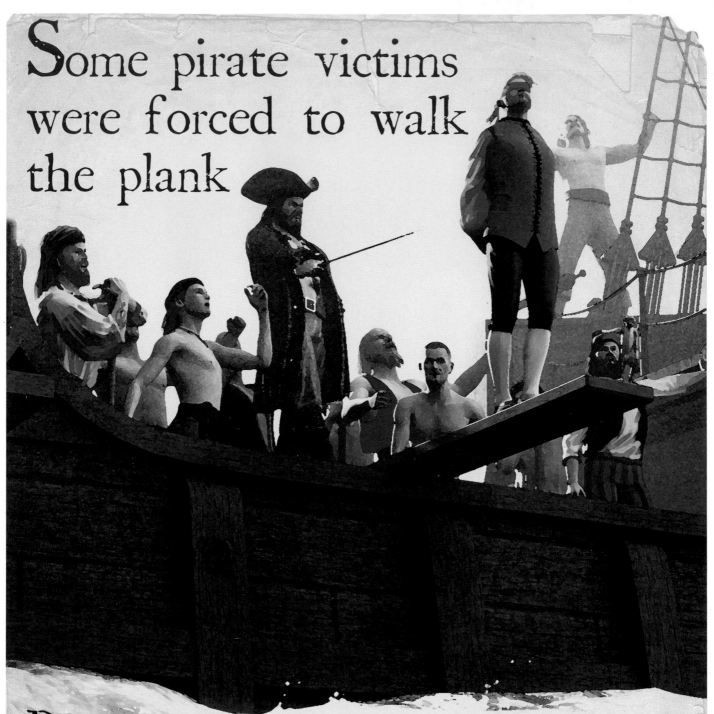

Pirates might make their **captives** walk the plank to scare them into telling where their gold was hidden. If the victims ended up in the water they drowned or were eaten by sharks. Walking the plank was quite rare though. Victims were usually just thrown overboard if the pirates had no use for them.

Pirates had rules

Most pirates had a set of rules called the **code of conduct**. They voted for who would be captain and could vote him out again at any time. There were no other officers since pirates hated to be told what to do.

One rule said no one could fight on board the ship. Quarrels had to be settled on land with a pistol or a sword. The **quartermaster** made sure the fight was fair. Usually a fight ended when one of the pirates drew blood.

Pirates shared their treasure equally

The pirate code stated that any **loot** had to be shared out equally. The quartermaster worked out who got what. This could be quite difficult when the treaure was made up of silks and jewels.

Gold coins were often cut up to make sure everyone got a fair share.

Some pirates were **marooned** on desert islands

If a pirate broke the rules he could be punished by being marooned. Usually he was left on a deserted island, often no more than a small sand bar at low tide. He would be given food, some water and a loaded pistol.

This often ended in death, but some men survived. Captain Edward England was marooned with two crew members on the island of Mauritius in the Indian Ocean. They built a raft and made it safely to Madagascar.

Pirates kept pets

Pets such as parrots and monkeys were popular with all sailors. Pirates in the Caribbean traded cloth and other goods for these **exotic** animals.

These exotic pets fetched high prices in Europe. This was especially true of the colourful parrots and macaws, which could be taught to say words.

Pirates liked to sing songs

The most useful members of the crew were the carpenters, **navigators** and musicians. Pirates loved a good song and a dance. They sang when they hauled up the sails.

The code of conduct decreed that musicians rested on Sundays. This was needed as crew members could ask a musician to strike up a tune at any time.

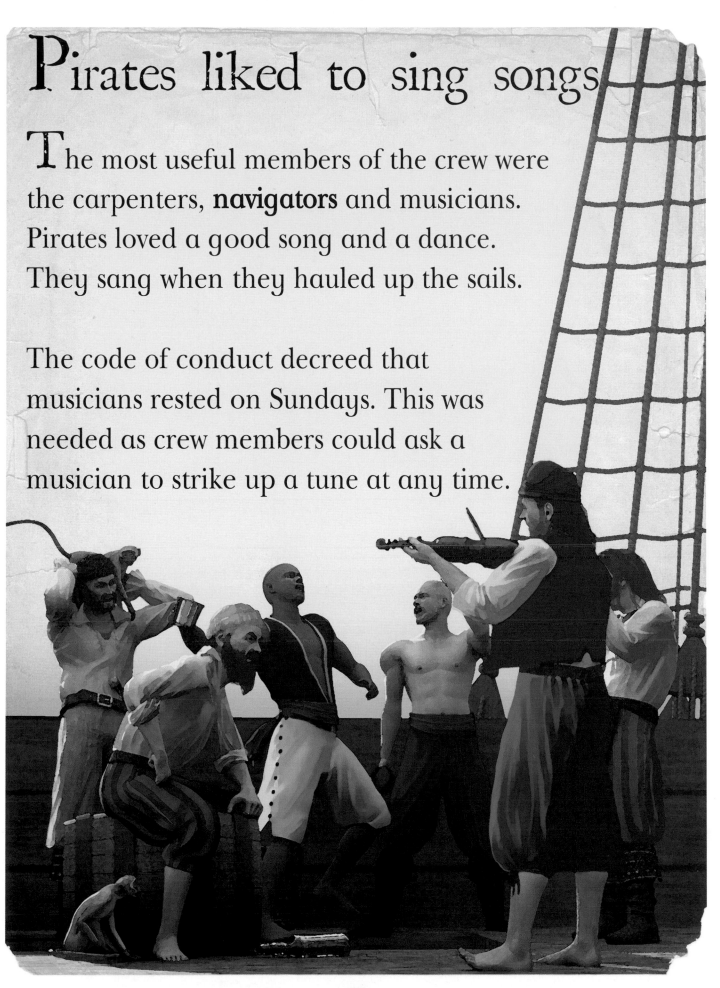

Some pirates went to bed at 8 o'clock

A pirate's day was long and hard. When the sun went down there was little to do except catch up on some sleep. The pirate captain Bartholomew Roberts's code of conduct number 4 was:

'The lights and candles should be put out at eight at night, and if any of the crew desire to drink after that hour they shall sit upon the open deck without lights.'

Pirates had injury **insurance**

Life as a pirate was dangerous. Pirates often lost a limb from cannon fire but many survived to tell the tale. Pirates donated some of their **booty** to help those who had been injured.

One pirate code of conduct stated, 'Every man who shall become a cripple or lose a limb in the service shall have 800 pieces of eight from the common stock'.

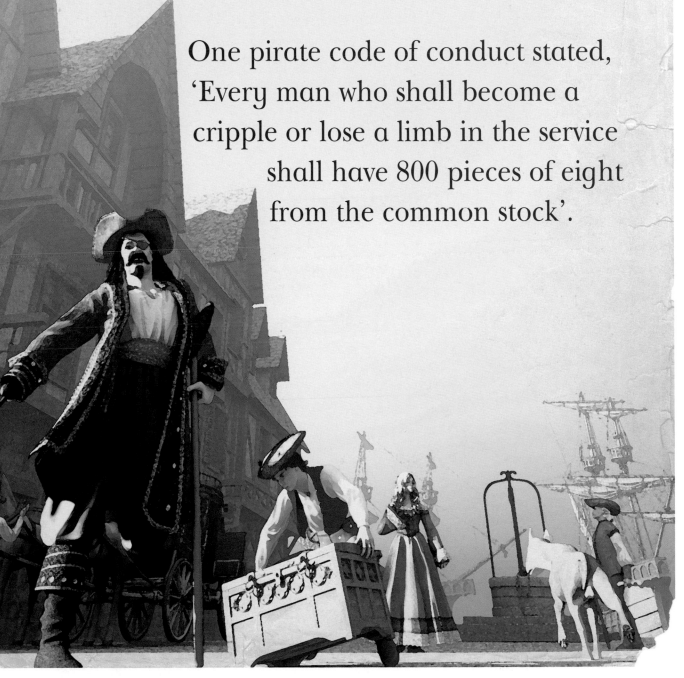

Some pirates had peg legs

The famous French pirate captain Francois Le Clerc was wounded fighting the English in 1549. He replaced his **amputated** leg with a wooden one. Le Clerc still led successful raids against the Spanish, who nicknamed him 'Peg Leg'.

He came to a sticky end in 1563 while attacking Spanish treasure ships.

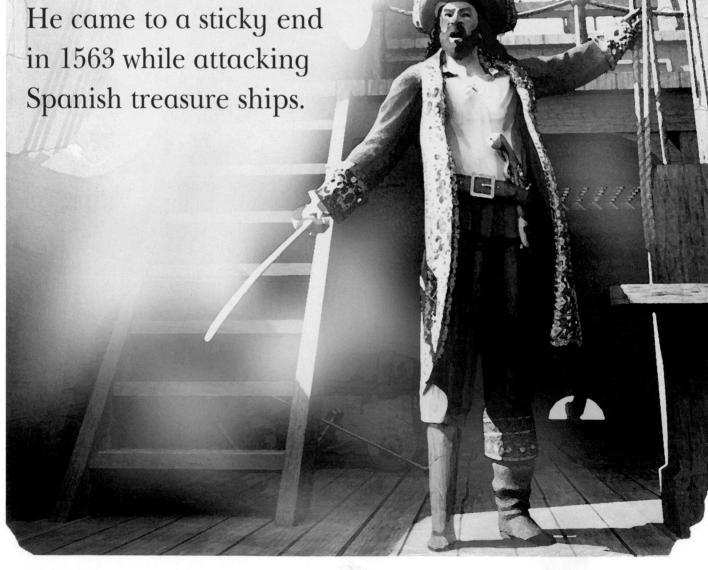

Black Bart liked to drink tea

Pirates drank lots of rum. In fact they drank any type of **liquor**. The famous pirate captain Bartholomew Roberts, known as Black Bart, was different.

Black Bart had a fearsome reputation and was one of the most successful pirates of all time. Although he sometimes drank a tankard of ale his favourite drink was a nice cup of tea!

17

Pirates buried their treasure

Pirate booty was usually food, drink and clothing. When they did get gold they spent it, although there are some stories of pirates burying their treasure.

Captain Kidd buried treasure on Gardiner's Island, near Long Island, New York. Most of it was found when he was arrested but people still hunt for the rest of it today.

Blackbeard's real name was Edward Teach

Blackbeard was a well-known English pirate. He attacked ships around the West Indies and the eastern coast of America from 1716 to 1718.

His nickname came from his large black beard. He twisted lengths of lighted fuse through it to scare his enemies when he attacked their ships.

Blackbeard's short career ended in 1718. He died after attacking British naval ships sent to capture him.

Not all pirates were men

Some famous pirates were women. Anne Bonny and Mary Read were members of John 'Calico Jack' Rackham's crew.

Both women wore men's clothing and were fierce fighters. They were captured in 1780 with Calico Jack and were sent to prison in Jamaica. Mary died in prison but Anne escaped and then disappeared without a trace.

Mary beat a fellow pirate in a sword fight

When Mary Read found out her boyfriend had to fight a dual with another pirate she feared he would lose. She insulted the other pirate so that he would have to fight her first.

When her boyfriend turned up to fight he found the pirate dead. Mary had killed him in a sword fight.

Mrs Cheng owned the biggest pirate fleet

Cheng I Sao (wife of Cheng I) and her husband ran a group of over 50,000 pirates. When her husband died in 1807, Mrs Cheng took command.

Their fleet consisted of 200 ocean-going **junks**, 600–800 coastal boats, and dozens of small river boats.

Glossary

amputated Cut off, often refers to a limb too injured to survive.

booty Another word for treasure.

captive A person who has been captured.

code of conduct Rules of behaviour.

creeks Narrow inlets in a shoreline.

draught The distance between the water's surface and the bottom of a ship.

exotic From foreign lands.

insurance Contract in which a group of people pay out money to others for a particular loss.

junk An ancient Chinese sailing vessel. Its design is still used today.

liquor A strong alcoholic drink.

loot Another word for treasure.

marooned Left trapped and alone somewhere inaccessible.

navigator An important member of a ship's crew who uses charts and experience to get a ship safely from one place to another.

quartermaster The second most important crew member after the captain.

Index